**And They Reached Out Their Hands
in Longing for the Distant Shore**

And They Reached Out Their Hands in Longing for the Distant Shore, poems © Peter Weltner 2022

All rights reserved

Marrowstone Press

ISBN: 978-0-578-29113-0

Cover image: Galen Garwood © 2022

And They Reached Out Their Hands
in Longing for the Distant Shore

Peter Weltner   poems

MARROWSTONE PRESS

stabant orantes primi transmittere cursum
tendebantque manus ripae ulterioris amore,
navita sed tristis nunc hos nunc accipit illos
ast alios longe submotos arcet harena.

    Virgil, *Aeneid*, Book VI, ll. 313-316

—and the dead stood praying to be the first to voyage over,
and reached out their hands in longing for the distant shore,
but the woeful boatman, Charon, chooses these and those
and fends off others, forcing them from the sandy strand.

*To Mary Madlin, My First Latin Teacher,
to Professor John Mattingly, Classicist,
and to the Memories of
William Chaplin and Joseph J. Hayes*

Table of Contents

I.

After Herakleitos 1
After Archilochus 5
After Three Papyrus Fragments 6
Fables of Ithaca 10
Plato's Metaphysics 11
The Philoctetes, after Sophocles 16
Antigone in Ukraine 18
After Euripides 19
Bright Apollo, after Euripides' Rhesos 21
Toward a History of Violence 23
Fasces 32
Exile 36
From a Lost Gospel of Mark 39
Parable of the Lost Sheep 51
Easter Monday Morning on Kure Beach, after Augustine 52
A Mind Too Fine to Be Violated by a Thought 57

II.

Purity of Heart Is To Will One Thing 61
Sweet Life, after Brahms' Vier ernste Gesänge 62
Sparrow 64
Rites of the New Year 65
December 7, 1941 67
Lvov 68
Three Degrees below Zero 69
After Listening to Bach 71
An Early Morning Walk on the Day after Christmas 72
Dreaming Homeward 73
A Poem Made from Poems Written When I Was Sixteen 75
Of Prayer 77
Company, after Stephen Sondheim 78
Rainbow 79
Immortal Gardener 80
Spring Sonata: The Light May Sees By 81

I

After Herakleitos
    Ηθος Ανθρωπος Δαιμων

    1.

Late in life, his nighttime mind remains composed of Greek
thoughts, rooted in the earth, wild rivers, the seas.
Fundamental things. Wherever a person might seek
to go to learn what he thinks, whatever it is life conceives
of as good. Say abandonment is the only way home.
Say silence is found, unsounded, in the depths of speech,
in the solitude of sages who, breathless, mutter, "Come.
Come with me," on their deathbeds. Who mean us to reach
an understanding of what it is that quiet has taught them,
why they say the past creates its own unmaking.
It is May. The woods smell of fresh sap and resin and loam,
wild flowers wayside on the hikes he takes, humming
an old song, I'd guess, from his contemplative look. See the stem
of a wild rose, studded with thorns, that a bee heeds the call
of? It tells him why all things change, what Meister Eckhart meant by All.

    2.

The flowers then, growing on the edge of the island,
bloomed like a woman with a fantastical head
of hair, her tresses like sirens'. Try to understand
what that might mean, not what anyone has said
before, but speaking of why the sun would make
its entrance daily, like us exploring more passionate
and dramatic lives, the gardens lush around a lake
so blue that a mind, attempting to contemplate
it for what it is, discovers only its own limitations
as if it had been attending to the cosmos or swept up
by the petals' thousands of sensual colors and pleasures.
I think of the precious things I've seen like revelations
with you, my love. A Doric column flecked with gold. A pewter cup
slightly tarnished. A wooden icon's amethyst eyes. The wisdom of years
passing before us like the island's temple of Hera its people no longer treasure.

3.

At Delphi, Apollo once said, "My oracles are liars."
Daphne flees the sun. Actaeon
and his dogs are made rabid by the moon. Desires
are like that. Seaside gray, a Mediterranean
storm looms. Lightning like waves. Ruins.
A bare, stony hill. A tower rising
behind it. Who wins?
A boy is dashing
through a field of blistered weeds.
Wearing torn, baggy pants, he runs to still his fear.
A smoky sky means fires are burning somewhere.
Every scene misleads
the seer to think what he has seen is real,
yet the troubling matter of life remains dissatisfied. Feel
this small pebble smoothed by rain, the wet fur of a Naxian
cat. Tell me what they mean. You, who sundered me in your golden godhead.

4.

Ethics like an old hermit not quite in sight
of the water he thirsts for,
waiting for what never was and never could be
to return before the last light
fails him, a drunk monk, perhaps, or a spiritual
fool like a crane
flying ever higher over the ridge of hills covered with tall
pine toward a moon glittering
like fishes' silvery scales in a pond near a lane
he has walked past often before, staring
into the wind-stirred pool
in search of the face his mind's
illusions mirror. No fool
he, then, led by the moon's reflection to play the blind
man and drown in its transient beauty.

5.

Love is born from water,
everything flows:
bodies light as air,
eyes lit by St. Elmo's
fire,
souls burning in their sorrows.
Earth is desire.
Two men, apart, walk down a pathway
each in search of the other.
They talk like people with little to say
of lives they no longer remember,
two ghosts whose bodies
will mingle into the same river some day
as its tributaries
flood the sea near the delta while the world is busy with summer.

6.

You despise silence, randomness, the rapidity
of change, though you say life moves
far too laggardly for you. Be
whoever you like, the past proves
stronger. History
is like a scar, you complain,
made of pain.
There's a shelf beneath
the Atlantic no one has found
yet, though it still affects the tides
like a reef
ships wreck on that hides
itself in storms. This is the wound
of the past you feel on your body,
you say to the sea. The grief you never can bury.

7.

In a grove that was partially burned
spindly pine trees stand
alone, one by one, stark, charred,
yet orderly.
The year has turned
to spring now. The land
so lately marred
by fires quickens.
A new geometry
re-composes the forest.
Surprisingly,
holiness often
begins again like these woods: shadows of what was there
before the lightning came remade into silhouettes that time
can mark its changes by.

8.

What if the beauty of the world were never spent?
However violently it was created,
suppose our love for it was what creation meant.
Near a broken oak tree, bent and splintered,
starlings preen on the grass, black,
spotted white, opalescent.
A man stands just far enough back
to listen to them sing. One starts.
The others follow. Snippets of a tune,
gentle, sweet. It brings joy to his heart.
It is news to no one that life ends much too soon.
Make of this fact an ethics if you can: the daimon
that sings inside humanity through a starling's throat,
warbling, trilling, chattering, whistling, stealing melodies
from other birds you, too, might learn to imitate, note by borrowed note.

After Archilochus

Cliffside, the smoke grows blacker, more acrid
from smoldering fires. Thrown
onto sand gray as flat slate
where the wind had skidded
along the beach by force of the surf,
his body naked, the men there famous, world known
for how easily they hate,
the taut, knot-haired men of Salmydessos
in Thrace where he lay among salvaged stuff
and booty on the springy turf
and sandy, thin-layers of duff
where its pirate-scavengers make the sailors
they save eat the bitter bread baked for slaves,
day after day the sky an imprisoning gray,
he, clothed in the mire of slime and seaweed, by the loss
of his freedom made abject, helpless, who perpetually raves
against his fate, the day
he was born, seen on the beach-break while the fog pours
in, the sea barely visible as another ship drifts westward
toward the rocks, clouds indistinguishable from the horizon
near where I pray to the gods, upon
an altar sacred to Poseidon,
that I be there to watch how hard
his life has become, for he did me wrong, and the morning,
shrouded in its mortal gray haze,
knows it, how many days
he inveighed against me and planted his heel on me, shattering
our faith in each other, he who long ago,
by the sweetly flowing Klaikos
and the wheat-bearing plain
of Mysia, would send
me to my grave as if among those slain
at the fall of Ilion,
at the end
of the war we'd fought in together, my friend.

After Three Papyrus Fragments

1. Xenophanes

Some questions need to be answered before
it is too late. But first prepare
the setting. In a bowl
arrange cut pink peonies,
red roses, and far more
lilies than he has ever seen. Place a ripe pear
and red apples on a porcelain dish. Let him feel the breeze
blowing through windows. Let the cooling air console
him, offer him comfort. Remark on the giddy,
wet dog frolicking outside, its joy
like yours when you were a boy
in Thebes. Chickadees,
titmice, finches on the wing, a wood dove in a tree,
gently singing. A peaceful scene. A white linen
table cloth, a bottle the sun shines through
like a rainbow, throwing a swath of prismatic colors onto
a plain wall. Drink wine, eat cake until it is time to ask, "Who
are you, in truth? Where did you live before it began?
How old are you now? How old were you then,
when the blood-bent tyrant ravaged our land,
laid waste to our city
and no one could know when the evil days might pass,
or what to call you, Pythagoras?"

2. Anonymous

Kyrnos, wherever men feast,
wherever men
gather for pleasure, beasts
of burden will take you.
Where flutes pipe of your fame,
by the Haliakmon,
there you shall be,
wide as the plain
and long as its course.

Though you roam in Hades
without a name,
no memories
of past things
you shall be happy.
Where fish swarm
near islands where all is warm
you shall find constancy.
Your deeds shall survive forever,
your fervor, ardor
recalled by us always.

Memory is desire,
hudor pyrá.

On Helicon, by the power
of metamorphoses
two streams,
Aganippe and Hippocrene,
sing all day of how
Aphrodite
was born not of Zeus
and the sea
but water set on fire.

You rode astride your wild-maned horse,
like Hippolitos incited by Poseidon's
curse,
jealous of his purity,
dragged into the sea
by his god-crazed team,
into the cleansing tides of Okeanos.
Kyrnos, a soldier,
floats dead in a river
turned
char-black
by water burned
and burning.

3. *Alcaeus*

The forestays weaken. All cargo
is tossed overboard.
Let us ride out the storm, though grim clouds hang low
over the horizon. Beaten hard
by the rising seas, no
ship can fight against the power of waves
when rival winds are set against each other
like men at war
that break apart on reefs.
What keeps
us alive, my friend? Best of all things is water.
Ariston men hudor.
Yet what god saves
us from what they call best? Soon, the dog star
will wheel in the sky,
bring back the parch of summer's
heat, cicadas' cries beneath the leaves,
artichoke flowers,
and battles that bring us to our knees.

Let us drink and be drunk forever, Melanippos.
Why aspire to be great?
Let us expect much from Dionysos
while we still are young and masters of our fate.
When the storm is over, torches will glow
near ports and harbors,
riotous with soldiers
at the end of their labors.
In every broken bit of darkness fallen,
our deaths await us.
On night's nether side,
all will be ashen and black,

as the sea is after barbarians attack
us. Let us pretend our war is over,
you the winner and I your prize.
Before sky and sea flow into one, before oblivion
descends upon
us and we must cross Acheron,
the river no one ever crosses twice,
look into my eyes.

Fables of Ithaka

Soon he must sail again on his fabled seas. You know
those he means. Clear deep waters, bronze sun,
Greek blue skies. The summer winds that blow
steer him homeward, though no journey is done.
No one returns home. Nor will the new port
be on any map. Where to, this last trip? His fellow
sailors are eager to travel, but he sails alone. Time's too short
to find the world he seeks for them and him both, to go
where human grief breaks like dawn over mountain
peaks and the men who died before him rise
out of the waters where they'd drowned in pain,
begging him to mourn them like soldiers who to his surprise
in Hades had to drink blood to speak. As waves lap like sirens'
songs enticing him from safety, his friends' ghosts fade. Dear companions,
he says to his dead, you dwell where dreams end, where imagination dies.

And yet he spies at twilight, in each final flickering flame
burning along the horizon, in the chill
night air, not how alike, how much the same
all voyages are, but the need still
to journey ever onward since, as if by fate's design,
the sun at dusk this day has shone
him on the night-darkened skyline
a light that is beckoning him not to familiar, but unknown
places—beyond earth
or sky, beyond mortality
and death's and birth's
failed vows—that he begin an endless odyssey
into the oarless desert of his heart
where memory is the only ocean left to sail on as if to start
on the final voyage is to embark on the past's as yet uncharted seas.

Plato's Metaphysics

1.

Beaches are good places to seek silence,
though waves crack like ice floes
breaking. Near sunset,
winds return with a deliberate violence,

like a grief one knows that never goes
away. Crumbling, destitute, wet
to the core, the seawall's
failing. A kitesurfer flies over the sea

where white caps leap far as the horizon.
A swimmer in a wetsuit crawls
out of the surf, exhausted.
Crows and gulls scurry,

caw or shriek as if mimicking a dirge.
Pounding waves surge
past the highway, sand-slicked,
sticky with seaweed. Why,

like the stillness abiding inside a terror,
does all go quiet
when you sigh, in breathless ululation
at the wonder of it, the muted abstention

of sense as if nothing belongs to time
now the other world's begun
and nothing, no one,
knows how to praise life in the ways of the sublime.

2.

A boy who has lost the good of his mind
but not his gaiety,
dances on a dune as if blind
to the tragedy his eyes see

clearly, the ghosts he evokes of,
oh, I don't know, some love
he once knew and lost
to the sea and its heaving waters.

    3.

If time's most painful powers are yet to come,
leave with me. Let's return home.
Seek comfort in heron, egret, snake,
plaited reeds and ferns, mist off the lake,

clouds dividing, re-gathering, black,
steely gray, battered, yet sheen
as satin or the smoke-stack-
ashen of velvet, creeks a phosphorescent green.

Let the great rain again flood farms,
pour down on our town. And on you
and me getting wetter, too,
since the storm harms

nothing important. Spillway. Bird wing.
Water lily. Oak tree. The world
as we knew it swirled
up in the beauty and thrill of lightning

on a summer afternoon, the throbbing air,
thunderbolts, rushing water,
gale-like winds: something of despair
in it, I suppose, but you and I were never happier.

    4.

Take care of your ghosts, I'm told. Offer them
common pleasures. They float over
the world wanting back in. At the beach,
a steel-like smell stings the air.

Salt dust encrusts sand, pebbles, rocks,
shards of crabs' shells. A crow pecks
at a fish's gutted, bony carcass.
A man in waders deftly casts his line.

Spray from high waves hovers over
the beach, gushes past walls,
splashes onto streets. Seawater
spouts from car tires as off boats' hulls.

A rust- and sulfur-colored foam
drifts, rolling like tumbleweed
across the sand, along the dunes,
wherever breezes blow it. The madness,

the fit of humanity is in the wind
as it grows fiercer once night darkens
enough for us to sleep before the storm,
like the coming of peace, passes silently westward.

    5.

At first light, some clouds are white like petals
of bay laurel, white like an old woman's hair,
like the eyes of a boy as he stares
at a bronze bird, at antique drinking vessels

in a museum, or the feathery white of dandelion
threads. Others are gray like ships beneath seas,
like wolf fur, chips in gravel pits, rain drops on stone,
faded linen, scabbards, or massive sheaves

of barn-stored grains shadowed from sunlight.
A few are black as fungus, cooled magma, onyx,
tar from pine rich with resin, ravens in flight
frightened by the morning, or as the river Styx

must be to carry us to our doom, I guess. At dawn,
they loom over a storm-endangered ocean
as if all the world were burning, the smoke drawn
heavenward like this morning's clouds, in premonition

of its ending, fires dampened, smoldering, or freshly lit
yet billowing, flowering, contracting, drifting,
through a sky whose sublimity we submit
to, the awe we yield to willingly, if devotion means anything.

6.

A metaphysic of mist,
the moon glowing
like a candle behind a scrim,
surpassing streetlights, hooded and dim.

A restless sea beats against
a craggy cement barrier
near where smoke from
a fire on the beach mixes with the drizzle.

Raccoons squabble behind
a wind-bowed silhouette
of a pine as a frail man with a cane
slowly clicks by unseen on the sidewalk.

A raven or a creature as hungry
scrounges through
a trash can. Coyotes howl
in the distant recesses of the fog.

Everything invisible is clearer if
left unspoken, silent
as this evening's whiteout in which
all the words one's said or written might vanish

into the bitterly cold, final embrace of cerecloth,
thought's cloak, the sun masked,
veiled too, haloed by mist as it sets, safe
to stare at unblinded until Truth burns through it tomorrow.

The Philoctetes after Sophocles

The wound, the bitter fate that's exiled
you to an island, to live in a cave,
putrescent, reviled,
where no one has come to save
you, though no victory at Troy
is possible without you, without your bow
at least, mere boy
oppressed by the weight
of fate,
like all those who know
the future, like a caryatid carrying upon
his shoulders the entablature
of a temple, bull-leaper, son
of the forest, of wilderness and rock, there is no cure
for what ails you, nowhere spared this endless war.

When the wind blows stronger, look east,
stare far off to where a man
will travel over the sea
to entice you, no priest
but a soldier besotted by hate, wine-dark
from shed blood, tan
from Ilium's sun
firing on its plains. Do not embark
on any ship with him. Shake
your unshorn hair like a bull's mane
and turn away. Do not mistake
his words for kindness. Step out of the light
for fear he might find you. You are lame,
hobbled, cannot fight.
Do not go. No war is ever won.

Stay hidden in the shadows of your cavernous
wound, though the early spring air
blossoms with its victorious
perfumes of pomegranate, jacaranda, laurel.

Yes, you might bloom handsome and fair,
hale and well
as a naked boy once more, ripe as the day
you were born if you allow
those who abandoned you to win in a rout
brought about by your weaponry. So the gods might say,
lying, smiling down in their ironic way
on row after row
of history's fallen, at all the lives lost
because of the cost
of the gift you gave the Greeks to save you of Herakles' bow and arrows.

Antigone in Ukraine

Spring is winter re-darkening. A hard wind blows
sparrows and swifts into the leaps and lifts of a dance

so that when they flap their wings, test their strength
against the air's force, they appear to fly nowhere,

though all is motion, all stays or goes as clouds
billow, smoke twists and tumbles to a tympanic

rhythm, the relentless beat of bombs over cities
while each explosion repeats, "Suffering never changes."

Antigone knows that for the dead any deed done
must be holy, must leave its sacred mark,

yet Creon chose power over awe and so he wails:
his, not their own hand will strike wife and son.

What honors the gods is piety. Yet men who disobey
their hallowed laws strut unpunished to their graves.

Annihilation is absurd, death is obscene, sears all
sense. Even the holiest body must rot to bone.

But, though dead when her cave's unsealed, Antigone
survives in story, legend, myth, tragedies, poems

of what the world is like, the force of a violence
that, cruel as winds in a storm, blows all away

and of the birds that soar over desolate fields, defiant
of gale or tempest, the brutal currents they must ride on,

while below, again, Antigone's led in sorrow to the way
that awaits her, the sacred eye of flame unearthing her death tomorrow.

After Euripides

> "The sea washes away all human evil."
> Anne Carson

1. *Agamemnon*

Murmurs of Troy-bound winds, the calm sea a mirror
of an ephemeral peace, another black freighter
on its way into harbor. The mountain near
the olive groves is bald as a church dome. Older
than the gods, wrapped in shawls darker than night, women
cross themselves in its shadows. At sunset,
it gleams and blesses no one. A small airplane
flies in new tourists. To find a few gold coins. A spangling trinket.
Pursue rumors of gold. I climb to the wind-sharpened rock
on the summit of a lesser mountain,
cup my hands in a pool of rainwater
to perform my morning ablution. On the dock
far below, fishermen empty their catch from their nets. Again
the net. You and I trapped by the same wide net, my daughter,
you god-doomed to be the soul destroyed and I your murderer.

2. *Iphigenia*

No, the god-stilled winds that becalmed your ships
blew on storm-strong inside you, father. The reason
you killed me—not to kidnap whore Helen whose lips
Paris had locked to his like a chain, who would shun
you and Menelaus like filthy swine if she saw
either of you again—was to prove how far blood-
lust could take you. So you slaughtered me. The law
never mattered to you. I was the daughter you loved
most. But you needed a war to rid you of the shame
the strumpet had brought down upon our family.
You longed to show how murderous you could be
to your men, to whip them into a frenzy. I am the same
as you now, the deer, whose blood you washed your hands in
thinking it me, is every stranger that transgresses the Taurians'
borders, each refugee from Libya, Syria that I'd sacrificed. Who died by sea.

3. Orestes

Made mad by Themis, the midnight dark earth mother
deep within me, oh Clytemnestra, I wage an endless war,
lawless furies tormenting me for your murder.
But I kill no enemies. Only oxen, cattle. The roar
I hear inside me is the thunderous voice of my terror.
Iphigenia, sister, look cliffside, by the beach where the slain
lie bleeding. Blood fills my eyes. I see only their pain.
Suffering. Your and my dead. Yet you are cleverer.
Save me and Pylades and yourself. Cleanse the stain
of who we are, free our family. Let us wash the icon
of Artemis and ourselves in the wise Aegean, in its purity.
You know best how to perform its rites against pollution.
The past is the last sacrifice we must make to please
the vengeful gods, to sail home at last, lacking nothing, happy at sea,
dreaming, as the Eumenides would have us dream, of a people's dreams of peace.

Bright Apollo, after Euripides' Rhesos

Right before dawn, a man dreams of an enormous cave,
a vast, carved out excavation in which those
who died without peace might dwell, not a grave
exactly, not a place meant for heroes
only, but a dimly lit darkness where life
continues at the extremes of the earth
by repeating each person's grief and strife,
all that has happened to them from birth
to death, in love and fear, joy and sorrow.
A place made of stone or lead or iron that's slowly
worn away by wind and water by order of necessity.
For the man had been reading Euripides' Rhesos
throughout night while waiting for the sun to rise at the moment,
the exact instant Trojans would attack the Greek camp: in the folly
of Hektor's delusions at dawn, with all the disasters of the wars to follow.

Defeat was inevitable once his spy Dolon in his wolf disguise was caught
and slaughtered, but not before he'd revealed
the Trojan's password. "Bright Apollo," a god who'd fought
on their side, yet no one, nothing has ever survived
the gods' duplicities. And Rhesos, king of Thrace,
most beautiful of heroes, of warriors, son
of a river divinity and one of the Muses, what trace
of him is left on earth, murdered by Odysseus
before he could fight on Troy's side? There is no truce
in the wars among gods, yet fate demands what is done
must be done divinely. Rhesos was never to see daylight
again nor receive Apollo's blessing but to dwell forever
in Pangaion's cavernous mountain. All children, his mother
laments, are creations of accident. Remember Rhesos, revere
him, for he is holy now, she says and prays, the daughter of Memory and Zeus.

So the play says, too, in its way. The man stares out his window. Suddenly
his long night is over. It was only a dream, as he
repeatedly says. Winds shake the branches of a tree
whose ripe fruit falls to the ground. He walks outside into
the little garden he and his lover cultivated, picks
up a plum, and wipes it on his sleeve. It tastes so
sweet it feels miraculous, like a gift from life. Yet what tricks
it inflicts on everyone, what confusions it sows is Euripides'
theme. The bay is green and shiny as a ripe olive.
A boat with yellow sails skates over choppy seas
that glitter like a summer purified by sunlight. Gods are secretive,
vindictive for no good reason. So be it. He misses
his lover, his friends, his happiness. Oh, Bright Apollo, dawning
in the east as birds buckle in the swift air like soldiers panicking
on Ilium's plain, you shine upon a lie-fraught land glazed and fired by morning.

Toward a History of Violence

I. 413 BCE

Bloated bodies are borne up daily out of the Middle Sea,
its waves strong as horses' haunches, whips of their manes,
groundswell and surge submerging skiffs, dinghies, reed
canoes, stolen or make-shift boats. Home lies lee-
ward, its shores abandoned, harborless. Storms, heavy rains
toss him off course as coasts dissolve, recede
into raging waters, steppes, plains like deserts
plundered by the war. His is the ancient migration,
the sea a wilderness, its howling waters, no rites sufficing
to change his fate or his city's history. Defeat converts
the losers to shades like those in caves sunlight shuns.
Alone, recalling by night a life that each day he's trying
to forget, he longs for a sign, the gull-billed tern
he saw on the morning he fled from Syracuse returning
from where it instinctively flew, eastward on its desperate sojourn.

II. 138-79 BCE

Gaius is dead, Lucius, noble companion, yours and mine, of our wars against Mithridates who slaughtered eighty thousand Italians, the Asiatic tyrant our dictator has let go, returned to power, promoted. Deceitful Sulla who after our victories marched on Rome to prevent the Italians from receiving the equality they had been promised.

What should we have expected of a man who had sacked all of Athens, looted Delphi's treasury, who'd bragged he had come to Attica not to learn its history but butcher its people? Believer in omens, oracles, visions, yet defiant of the gods. Killer of Roman citizens who'd resisted his power on the Esquiline Hill.

He who displayed Sulpicius' head on the Rostra. Who had an elderly neighbor and friend who had broken with him tossed from the Tarpeian Rock. Who at the Circus of Rome massacred a thousand Samnites whose dying cries echoed through the Temple of Bellona while he smugly lectured terrified senators on his great victories in Pontus.

How many did he slay? Sixty? A hundred bloodied white togas? Sixteen hundred equites? When did it begin, the fall of our Republic? Long ago, I suppose, the day two generations before us when Tiberius Gracchus was clubbed to death in the streets of our city.

"Quit quoting laws to us," says Pompey, "who have swords to wield." Restless legions have replaced the Republic, Lucius. Our Gaius is dead, my friend. And like him for whom he was named, Gaius Gracchus, I mean, Tiberius' brother, he dies again and again.

What have we lost? Mos maiorum, the way of the elders. Customs, unwritten rules, communal hopes and dreams, bonds we Romans let be placed upon us, accepted for the good of the state we'd inherited.

No more civitas, suffragium. No more consuls, tribunes. Only Sulla, executor of the laws he has dictated, he claims, not for himself, not to enrich anyone, but to restore the ancient Republic, the old city, the old sacred Rome, the old laws he has revived by maintaining through his endless lies a new brute order of violence.

III. 37-68 CE

Dreams. Fire on a lake. The sky bleeding rain,
waves sinking triremes as an Apennine mountain
rises from slaves' skulls. I've circulated a list
of my enemies' names. A praetorian shakes his fist
at them like a gladiator, like one of the Myrmidons
amassing at the Skaian gates. Why fear the sons
of the men I've disposed of? I watch Neoptolemus
lobbing heads over walls. "No one kills like us,
Caesar," he says. Nonsense. I call for Poppaea,
my cock-licking pussy-snatch, for Agrippina,
my derelict mother. My shipwrights built a gold boat
for her to wreck in. A rickety tower. Quote
me, please. Publicity contents me. I'll sing in Attica,
perform my drag act. "What genius. Pulchra carmina,"
they'll respond, fools swooning overseas. Seneca,
my sage. You abide by the precepts of the stoa,

you claim, but you're rich as Croesus. "Fop, clown,"
you call me, don't you? But to my face you frown,
protesting. "Antic player, over actor. Stagey."
Lucius. I know your plots. I hear what you say.
My spies tell me what everyone thinks. So I've burned
the city and its riffraff down while I insouciantly tuned
my lyre to sing of its ruin, blaming it on that atheist
cult I had tarred and torched alive. What a feast
for the eyes. Why should I worry about what history
might say of me? Fake news! Lies! My sanity
doubted by Suetonius, Tacitus? Who cares? I wield facts
like a soldier his sword, a gladiator his ax.
Yet I cannot rest. The earth's a nightmare of omens
and prophecies. Dead at the hands of Romans.
"Vindictive, unscrupulous fool," those two will declare
in their books. Yet I do what any ruler must dare
to do. I pursue the politics of rage. Of cruelty.
The revenge I gladly take on all who fail to love me.
Suppose a life were only a bad dream that never is true
not even once, but revives itself, like me in you,
endlessly. I'd be as safe as any man ever in power.
And my people, sleeping blithely, insanely happy hour after hour.

IV. 1919-1922 CE

The docks are packed with people, boxes, pets,
livestock. The night's been frantic. The rising sun
wounds the Mediterranean. They hear gunshots
close by that mean to terrify. No one Greek gets
to stay. The boat they ride in is set upon
by Turks who throw men overboard. One rots
on the deck. The skiff passes Chios, the sea
the exiles sing of like the ancient bards of tragedy.
They roam the islands, the Peloponnesus. Like goats,
they nibble on thistles and weeds. A white-washed church
rings its tower's bells in mourning. Below, the water

steams volcanically. The sky's Aegean deep. Throats are parched,
feet blistered. Someday, others will search these plains, mountains for
their bones, teeth from the grave they were sealed alive in by history,
each an Antigone desperate in her cave.

V. 1939-1945 CE

1. Berlin

And schoolchildren reciting patriotic poems, windows
flung open, singing hymns as they march into
destiny, praising the war's many heroes.
All calumnies against the nation have proved untrue.
And the broadcasts every family raptly listens to, no
matter the hour while our Leader speaks
to denounce the dangers from the East and its low,
beast-like, vile hordes who stink of turnips and leeks.
I've heard what others say, read what they write in
newspapers, but it's propaganda, foreigners' lies.
It is not wrong for a country, neither evil nor a sin,
to favor its own race. Terror is the course of the wise.
It is not wicked, our treatment of Jews and gypsies,
sodomites and the genetically mad or ill-fit. A rusty, dull
knife cuts nothing. Only violent men survive. Seize power. Be joyful.

2. Tuchola Forest

My childhood was a wolf's, spent
among wolves in the silence
of a forest. I bent
birch trees for the leaves to sleep on,
my disappearance
never noticed. I say I won
when the king
of wolves chose me first, selected me for
his special child, gave me his ring

to wear that I adore
as only a wolf cub can. I explore
in woods for my lost brothers–
the ring in my ear of silver and the gold teeth he tore
from my mother
who loved me less than the she-wolf I was ripped from like a stranger.

3. Prague

Innocent books like people are banned, forbidden,
then disappear. He secures his desk drawers,
the latches on his windows, knows when
it'll be too late to leave: bootsteps on the floors
above his own. Down the hall, a shout
of hatred shocks him into silence. What
must he do? He's read the paper, all about
the dangers. An old, tired bookseller, yet that
alone might doom him. He imagines himself
tortured in a cell, on a steel cot, a man, like him,
of imagination, a purveyor of books, the wealth
of every nation. Buzzing, whirring, strident, grim,
the terrifying sirens sound. It's the round-up again.
A knock on the door sets a bonfire blazing in his brain.
As bright as books in a fire, his mind burns from the rifle's butt.

4. Trzesn

Her village is no more, all its inhabitants
dead or fled weeks ago. Her labor
is never done. She works in a trance,
keeps the shades down, gathers fresh rain water
in unwashed bottles, craves a hole
to hide in like a snake. There is no one
left who might atone for it, console
her for it, the grave-like bed she sleeps in alone.

Who was the soldier who broke her world
into rubble and laughed as it crumbled into
dust? She once had loved to flirt, being twirled
on the dance floor, gossiping, singing, a new beau
on both arms. And then he appeared, the soldier
who'd shoot her later, shouting love-words for her to hear
while tanks rolled in, crushing to the dust her street's cobblestone.

5. *Kortelisy*

The house was no refuge for him and his dear friend,
loving as a brother, whose wounded head was bandaged
poorly. At least he died in a bed. What gift could dawn send
them tomorrow? Only in the dark had they managed
to survive. Neither spoke of how the two
of them had nearly perished nor why they'd almost
deserted. Yet not even darkness might be through
with them. See? Each is becoming a ghost
to the other. No one is spared. Fog, snow, rain,
mud. And these few brief moments in a room
where no comfort will come for them. A window pane,
cracked and shuttered, whistles in the wind, "Soon,
soon." It is an ill omen of weather for the wind to blow
so hard, to rise and fall like waves in a lake. A throw
of the dice is what history is, he thinks. The lives of others, the life he's lost.

6. *Galicia*

No more soaring, gliding on the wind. Each dawn
silent as dead water or a field waiting for rain
to fall. None comes. No singing. No music.
They are gone. Geese. Grebes. Coots. Cuckoos.
Doves. Crane. Raven. Nor men, women,
children left to hear them. No bird call. No swallow
or wren in bush or brush. No robin. No
chirping, cheeping, warbling, cawing. Just
the waste of days, the long days without song,

silenced by your silence, testimony to the wrong
you did them. No more bird cry. Just you,
my friends, abandoned amid the ruins of nature. Denied
their flying. Just you and your sin to blame, my people,
on this clear day I give you to see, in your shame, your emptiness,
your misuse of me who held you in my bosom so long, so hushed and lovingly.

7. Berlin

A bitter moon, mustachioed and ruddy. Hump-
backed women wearing tattering shawls
rummage through the ruins of buildings,
their aprons so full of litter their bodies swell

like Sarah bearing her miraculous child.
Boys beg by the gate to the park, watch
a soldier drunkenly zigzagging down
a street only to stumble on a charred beam.

Dust has settled on the rubble. His pockets
picked, they kick him senseless. In the shell
of a house, an elderly man wraps himself
in a rug but cannot stop shivering in the cold.

His once strong hands are soft as pudding.
Famished, he crawls from under his useless
cover. The bleeding soldier lies crumpled
on the street. Foraging though his clothes,

the old man finds a coin the boys had missed
but cannot keep it from their thieving
hands or the knife that slices his wrist.
Their shouts of triumph over his body

sound to his exhausted ears almost innocent
now, like the moon-besotted howling of wolf cubs
as they trap in the woods for food an old
sick hound too weak in its haunches to flee.

8. Rome

The last armies waded ashore before sunrise and went
unresisted. Sometimes, around camp fires, they
sang their new songs. Sometimes they were content
to let the people try to sing them, the joys they convey
more fervent than the soldiers' own. The hundred
words for pain were banished from plays and movies,
the thousand for loss stricken from speeches. During the dread-
filled days of the war, though silenced, some had fled
to safety to tell, to those who would listen, their stories.
But in a few years, the fate of states, once feared, became
normal, natural even, like another part of the landscape
or like a flower rendered more beautiful by giving it a new name.
And the children, marked and marred by war, were set out daily to die,
floating off in their little boats with only the youngest daring to cry,
knowing that peace had come too late to save them from their country's shame.

VI. 1972 CE

Suppose it were possible that myths could be real,
our fictions as true as you and I are, as readers
are when they believe in a story, in their hearts feel
the lives writers make up, all inveterate dreamers,
that it happened–the virgin birth in a barn or a cave,
angels singing of a child to shepherds, wise men
wending their way from the distant east, braving
dangers, bringing gifts, kneeling sheep and oxen–
that a fable could replace the violent Christmas day
when I was thirty and lived in the country far
from town and had quit the party inside to explore
the earth for auguries of peace, what birds might say
by traces left in snow as the wind blew and they soared
out of sight and bombs fell on 'Nam to end the war.

Fasces

1.

Devotees of Cybebe, brute, mindless power, now come
unbidden to, forbidden by Rome,
the city they would destroy.
sounding their lutes, drums, timbrels,
crotales, imbibing wine, bleeding. Nothing's
denied them. Theirs is the drunken joy
of desecration. Playthings of the irrational. Cabals,
wild beasts, rampaging from circus to forum
like conquering Gauls
in this city of decrepit old age,
of ghosts, visitations,
fears, premonitions, lies, and misprisions,
allowing every violence,
every expression of resentment and rage.
What now, senators, do you make of your cowardice and silence?

2.

So many of our companions have been slaughtered, Rufus.
Sylvester, Demetrius, Marcus, Felix.
At the end, their battle-weary bodies turned pus-
yellow, ice-blue, limbs stiff as marble and cold, pricks
sheathed and death-shriveled. And the terrors,
later, of the crucified eyeing us, their executioners,
while hawks and vultures ravenous
for carrion, the bleeding flesh that lures
them ever closer, slowly circled above the dying,
clacking their beaks like jaw bones rattling.
There is no Roman victory that is not ours
to suffer and confess to, Rufus, the shock of history
excoriating our bodies like the army at the siege of Carthage
long before our time, it's true, but with the same carnage
all empires display when led to embrace war's passions and cruelty.

3.

Now our cohort prepares to leave unhappy Rome to fight
once more on the Dacian border. Catullus
refused to say to Juventius what I must
risk my life by telling you, though the rite
we attended, our blood sacrifice to Bacchus
might yet protect us. You and I, Rufus,
must become traitors to power, emperors,
the imperium, doomed anyway as we are to be dust
beneath the feet of strangers, enemy warriors
who will trample upon us. From Brundisium, let us sail
to the shores of the Caspian sea, where the sun
rises each day lusty as you out of our bed. Let our wars
be over, Rufus. Is it not fascistic, violent to be Roman
in the world it's forged from marble, stone, steel by force of male
will? Spill wine on my body, Rufus, lick it. Let us fuck like the fairest of traitors.

4.

Along the craggy shoreline
where our days have ended,
I pour the sacred wine,
the libation you said
was mine to choose that you might rise
out of waves, from the cries
of island birds, to sail on a sea that would buoy you
westward to join your fellow shades. I've honored the rite,
your plea never to be forgotten, my brother. So
I vowed to you two
thousand and more years ago,
we both citizens of Rome, our eternal city,
while waves rocked you, crazed by fever, wanting water,
to sleep sleeplessly in my arms, on the last dim night
of history. Yet listen. How they march again. The fascisti.

5.

Medes overcome. Barbarians,
Gelonian bowmen
pacified by ten
years of fighting. Centurions,

lovers, battling Goths in wolf-toothed
forests. Armenians
across deserts who, massive as loosened
boulders, fell on us from snow-peaked mountains.

Lion-maned Parthians
womanly
armored in baggy trousers. Set-faced Egyptians.
Dolphin-sleek sea-

people. Boar-bold warriors
in oak-dark Germania.
Stone-hard, naked berserkers
in moon-maddened Britannia.

What, now that you are dead,
do I make of victory,
Rufus, though the world be pacified
and the great sea

freed of pirates? At the end of empire,
on the shore of the Mediterranean,
in searing heat, I tire
of temple and altar, all Rome's army's done.

Look at me. You'll find my hair
has grown white as a senator's.
toga. I fail to savor,
to delight in what wine I dare

drink. A wind storm
rattles the sand.
All men come to harm
is the sum of what little I understand.

At the end of the world, the limit
of reason, at water's
edge I am weary in spirit.
At night, I listen to the tellers

of tales, the bards of this desolate
place sing of history's
disasters as if insensate
to its pain. It is not tragedy's

way to speak of how I kissed
your lips, sun-warmed, inviting,
my blood quickening
into love, or how I've missed

you since you died.
The women here
wear black all year
to show that they've survived.

Exile
    P. Ovidii Nasonis mors

  1.

A man, a poet, an exile, stands on
a deserted shore
of Augustus' Mediterranean
empire, no more
temple, no more altar beasts
being slaughtered for the feasts
to follow, roast boars on slaves' shoulders
brought to table, no more courtesans
perfumed with scented waters,
garlanded with hibiscus and grape leaves
as Caesar savors
his poems about the metamorphoses
of all things even as his soldiers
fight his foreign wars
for power's sake and die and die as he might do for poetry
or the pleasures of Bacchus,
dancing to timbrels, flutes, drums, crotales, the muses'
music and joys and lusts in all their sensual inconsequence.

Nonsense
is the stuff poetry is made of if it never dares
to defy its Caesars.
Along this craggy shoreline
his days will end, ceded
to Augustus. Let him, then, freely pour the wine, the libation
that might induce to rise
out of the waves, at the cries
of seabirds, the sight of the ship
that would carry him homeward, at last done
with his punishment. A small boat a fisherman ties
dockside rocks like a cradle.
He is a teller of tales, of the ancients tragedies,
of how everything is metamorphic, changeable
save this: that all men come to harm, their lives suspended,
ended forever whether on the Parthian plains
or the Dacian borders

or by the Black Sea in the lands of unlatined barbarians.
City of decrepit old age,
of ghosts'
visitations,
lusts,
fears and premonitions,
lies and misprisions,
abiding every violence,
resentment, rage,
tell me, he longs to say,
how safe do you feel today, Rome,
hidden, even as you pray
behind the walls of your Olympian
silence
that death not come
for you like playthings
of the gods, of cabals
and plots, assassins from circus to forum
to end like me, an exile shuffling among lemures a thousand miles from home.

2.

In an open field by a desolate olive
grove, he found a shard he's pocketed
for luck. No one can live
forever, but might his poetry be read
down through the centuries? He eats melons,
figs, dates, and little more.
When he dies who will pour
wine on his grave
as an oblation, offer lemon cakes and honeyed almonds?
Wave after wave
laps at his feet. The ancient
Greeks believed that every language
begins in mourning, ululations, nothing lent
you, all you borrowed taken from you. Say poetry is a bandage

applied to conceal the suppuration,
the oozing of your wounds. Then grieve for the dead
none living can understand, the battle that goes on and on
in the heart even after death. The dread there is no end to it. The carnage.

This is where reading ancient poems brings us: to an island
where poetry began,
an ancient woman, black hair sun gritty,
a cracked-faced craggy fisherman
bound to the sea's cruel life,
both of whom know they must weep
as they laboriously climb steep,
zigzagging paths up a hill to the cemetery,
the place where tragedy
originated, to reach the meaning the exiled poet sees
as his own and yours and mine too, the old woman dressed
head to toe in night black, the fisherman limping, staring
out, out, beyond sight, both blessed
by a final vision
that shines far past the horizon, the dying half light
from the soul of devotion,
the common pain, the daily primordial suffering you write
us of, Ovid, a bitter wind chilling your eyes and the dead you see unchanging.

From a Lost Gospel of Mark

1. *A.M.D.G.: Advent*

A boat with a single sail slides across the sea. Waters part. A late dawn wind rustles the rushes along a wide shore. The blunted bulk of an ox heaves awake. In search of dew-wet twigs, a ram bounds from rock to rock. Snake, lizard lick desolation from the sand. Hermit-hived bees fly free. The Galilee's cold as ghosts' breath. Repairing nets, even a host of fishermen won't wade in. Locusts flying over head rattle like wind-tossed palms before a dust storm. Where no one dares to look, the head-high reeds divide for him and the sun that walks like a lover by his side.

2. *A Parable of Secrecy*

"Teacher, why do you speak in mysteries?"

"Lest they understand me and so be saved."

Crushed flat and boneless, a squirrel's pelt lies on the white line. The road's shoulder, crumbling into a tangle of kudzu, sweats tar. The trees' dry leaves shade what they can. A man parks his car on a stretch of packed clay. A path begins out of nowhere, leading through lush under brush and tall cane into the woods' spare light where fern and bark moss sparkle next to a boulder, pocked and worn as an old shoe heel. The path to the creek zigzags down slick red clay, its steep bank thick with pink and white rhododendron.

Gnats swarm over the trickling water where skates dart frantic as trapped flies. He can see the cave where, years before, a child, he dragged the body, its face slashed, its flesh torn, a rust red wound in its side wider than a bullet hole. But he looks no further. In the clearing beyond the woods, a dirt road curves along a field, the dry corn only hip high. Yellowed, stained, a farmhouse's shades are drawn, its old paint curled like wood shavings. A sallow woman answers his knock and with a long wood spoon points to an ancient plank bridge. When he reaches it, thirsty, he scrambles down the bank and kneels on a rock. Reflected by the creek, his face scares him. He cups some water to his lips. It tastes like brine or blood still seeping downstream from that bad old dream he cannot forget.

Real or not, what's done cannot be undone, no slaughtered lamb unslain. He swallows, washes his face, and, cooled, refreshed, walks on. With luck, he'll reach his car, and home, by noon.

3. *Clothes Like a Dove*

City folk. A car idles at a bridge. Its driver in a dust coat fetches water for two ladies wearing broad brimmed hats, their lace veils sewn with roses. As they drive off, the wheels splash mud on the boy's coveralls. He washes them in the river where he waits for hours, hoping to hear above on the old planks the drumming of their tires as they return from touring a lake's breaking ice.

Her son refuses to smile. His hair glitters with sawdust. His forearms are tapered like a baseball bat. He leans on a garage door that's weather-worn and over-grown with wild roses and vines. The sun glares in his eyes. In the photograph his mother snaps, they look black, suspicious as a bird's. A rip in his coveralls reveals a worse hole in his drawers. His pale hair blurs into the flare of his shiny shirt.

Dust clogs his nostrils. The air tastes like tin. The tobacco shrivels into weedy stalks. The corn looks trampled. The hens have quit laying. The cows' ribs protrude like posts. His older brother develops a cough one night, dies the next, grown so thin so quick his daddy must bury him in his younger son's clothes. The boy steals his brother's old torn jacket to wear at the funeral.

"Live shall your dead for your dew is the dew of light and Sharon's land shall give birth." The preacher kneels, fingers the earth, crumbling it, scattering it like seeds. A wind topples his bowler off his head into the grave where Father's shoveling dirt in fast, a hundred times quicker than it took to dig. Home, the boy takes a hat off a hook and tries it on for size.

His ears ache. His vomit is cow-cud green. He hides in a closet. When his father sticks the hog its squeal pricks the boy's eardrums like a pin. The slaughtering done, his dad showers off the blood as the boy tries on his father's drawers, wearing them round his neck like a bandanna or on his head like a baseball cap. His old man's slap spins his head like a sudden snap in crack-the-whip.

He carves creatures from wood—lifelike doves, titmice, blackbirds, orioles. But wood-en ones won't fly by themselves. His mother owns a fur-lined cloak he wears as Superman or wraps round his birds so that they some day might soar in the sky. He'd like to see them twirl faster and faster in smaller and smaller rings until, sun-bright, their flight would blind the sight of every unbeliever.

Woven from cotton or wool like clothes, carved from hard wood or soft, chiseled from stone or marble, moulded like clay, wrought like a poem from words, the body rises to paradise dressed its best, light as dove's feathers, the boy's mother says as she knits him a pullover warm enough for any winter storm that might rage yet that year. No need to fear the iciest cold, she says, wearing so loving a sweater.

4. *The Hem*

Twelve years a bleeder, unclean, the woman presses ever nearer as the mob recoils, recedes. Her fingers tremble to touch a fraying, dusty hem of his heavy cloak, too warm for such a sun. Yet, a seamstress herself when young, she knows, even trusts in the virtues women sew in clothes, especially those as coarsely woven as his, which somehow still adorns the man before whom she cowers, who calls her daughter, her gushing blood dried up by the miraculous power of his new testament, to which she testifies: Metonymy, beloved son.

5. *Loaves, Fishes*

Lost, stolen—the old man could no longer remember—gone, impoverishing him for good: the ruby cut like glass to form a tiny oval window through which his master could peer so that the day he slit his wrists wine-soaked happy Brundisium would look through his stone as bloody as the bowl Gaius had given him.

Once he owned thirty goats. Now road dirt, dust on his feet were his household gods, no weaker than the ones he'd swiped from his master's mantel. He squats in a fig grove. His bloody stools stink and steam. Figs cramp his guts worse than seeds or nuts. Spirit birds fly near the moon whose light each night unweaves more threads from his threadbare life, his only shelter caves that lie too near where the dead sleep, shuddering like lashed slaves he would have forgiven had their cries, screams not ruined his rest.

Take, eat: loaves, fishes. Strip off your sackcloth. Do not hide your faces. No longer deceive the Lord your God. Wear new clothes. Love your neighbor as yourself, you who will leave me one by one.

However much the crowd devours, the basket never empties. He grabs more grub than he can eat to save for hungry days ahead. Naked except for a tattered loin cloth, a boy leans against an old oak god, its thinnest roots thicker than his arms. His nose's been gnawed, his tongue's a stub, his fingers nubs. Careful not to touch his sores, the old man cracks open his pouch to offer him a taste of fish. The boy struggles to eat, swallows, and chokes on a bone. The old man pounds on his back hard until he spits it out. The sliver on his finger is as white as a tooth from an old ivory comb, the last of his master's things he'd sold.

No more fish for the boy, but instead just bread soaked soft in wine he can easily steal from a crowd weary from too much food and talk, like his master at his last meal, leaving behind so many fine bottles never drunk.

6. *Transfiguration*

A misty mountain top, sun dazzled by a song of sorts. A fugue perhaps whose cold strict parts resound with a fiery tune. How hear it now? How could any choir sing it? Any gong, bell, celeste, flute, fife, clarinet, oboe, zither, sitar, lyre, pipa, biwa, all of the Concertgebouw together play it? Had dust-covered men ever beaten it on deer skin drums? Black-clad women, tossing seeds on graves, wailed it, tearing the air? Had any bard intoned it after battle? In the Negev holy men, in Compostela's narrow streets pilgrims chanted it? Did viols perform it as a courtiers' pavan? On what village green, beneath what shell, had a band played it as a march for soldiers in gray or blue? Did Grumiaux tune his fiddle to it before he played Mozart or Bach? Did Corelli warm his voice to it before he sang E lucevan le stelle? Do birds, their hearts light-quickened, warble it at noon? Or wolves howl its agonies at the moon?

The song is lost to us like strands of the sun. Yet deep in a forest, a plain bright eyed little girl, centuries dust, still hums its tunes as she picks up pretty pebbles and gathers nuts to please herself and comfort us.

7. *Lazarus*

The hotel's abandoned, shut down. He locks the door to the lounge. Listening to storm reports, he washes cocktail glasses behind the bar. Each one he's dried, he places on a plastic shelf that runs across a mirror he's never looked in, scared of the dead man he'd see at fifty-three, afraid to count the days until, one by one, they're gone again. Restless, he's waiting for a call but won't pick up the phone, numbering each time it rings as just one more he has to hear before it's really over, his heart unable to bear another loss. The brutal winds shake the building, bouncing the bar's tables and chairs around as if an earthquake, not a hurricane were breaking the island apart.

He tastes ash on his tongue and swills some Cuban rum he keeps stashed beneath the cash register. A hundred burning huts make their own storm he'd learned as his best friend ran amuck after their platoon had lit them all, screaming he deserved a goddamn medal some lieutenant had deprived him of, then shooting chickens, pigs, gooks before he blasted his head off his neck with a grenade that killed them all. Only Marcus had survived, brought back from the dead in a field hospital, still gripping his best friend's dog tags.

He wears them around his neck like an amulet. After he's rinsed another glass in the soapless water, he wipes it with a fresh towel and inspects it for spots by the absinthe green light that fills the room as the dying winds chill the air. The chain around his neck feels tighter than it's ever felt before, Danny's tags weighing on his chest heavy as a shield. As he falls, he can't pull them off. Is his zippo out of fluid? Danny hands him his. For once a hut burns fast enough, as the enemy flees from the flames in his brain while their animals bellow and squawk.

8. *The Ficus*

He bought me in Laguna Beach where I'd been properly raised from a seed and grown content to stay in a house that was much too dark and lacked any views to speak of, though I was pleased by the ceiling I could touch if I chose. What man attends to a tree's forebodings?

He should have stayed put, but he thought he needed new friends, new lovers, and moved in search of them to a cramped cottage parked on a hill overlooking the seedy orange glow of Silver Lake. Shoved indecorously into a morose corner of the dining room, I did as I pleased. Out of spite, I dropped all my leaves and almost died.

At more than one party, drinks were drained, cigarettes snuffed out in my pot soil. I bore the affront like a stoic. As trees measure time, only a trickle or two of sap had passed before one afternoon I heard weeping on his bed. For days, he abandoned me without the least concern for my fate. In a pique, I plopped all my leaves on his floor and cared not the least when he walked through his door with one arm less.

He never bothered to sweep. I was sure he had sold me cheap to the cottage's new owner when he moved back south to Laguna. But, like a saint, he forgave me my sins and gave me back my corner.

I decided to thrive even as he grew thin, lost hair, coughed up gobs of red phlegm. But when he cursed God for all his misery and swore great oaths defying heaven, I shed my leaves in shock onto the decorative prayer rug that was still littered with them when Ricardo found him in a pool of blood. If I'd known his distress, I'd have made less of a mess. But goodness itself, Ricardo took me into his home anyway, setting me up on Catalina's better stretch, where the light is right and the view, well, the view is wide and almost satisfactory.

9. *The Fig Tree*

A damp wind blew along the Bethany road through the grove. I huddled among the other trees, neither the spindliest nor the hardiest, my branches criss-crossing, tangled with the others, my leaves' sharp frond shape dully green, my bark marked with tumors. Still low in the sky, the sun was barely ruddy as he and the twelve passed by taking no notice of us until he turned to one and declared he hungered out of season after figs and demanded of me some fruit to eat who had no figs to offer.

Whereupon, out of all reason he raged like a thwarted lover and cursed me for my fruit-lessness that had left his hunger deep, unsatisfied. Before sunrise the next day, I withered away, unlike the tree far less innocent than me he never cursed.

Make of me an image in your poem, a symbol in your sermon. Write an edifying allegory of me as type of all who deny their Lord. None of it matters a fig, as they say, to me anymore who am nowhere to be found, neither dust in the air nor dust in the ground along the route he took from Bethany to Jerusalem, working his famous miracles, just or not.

10. Judas's Fate

One son fights in France, another for years in New Guinea. A brother serves in the Balkans advising the OSS. In a week or so, a nephew will be out of hospital at last. He's ordered his wife, two daughters to dress always in black as they knit soldiers socks, sweaters, warm caps.

Mornings, he reads the news. In the afternoons, he listens to dispatches on the wire-less. Nights, he scans the skies for enemy planes. Children have risen against their parents before, brother has betrayed brother. But he will not flee to an inland refuge.

Let the bombs fall. Let no housetop not burn to the ground. He abhors dawn. It is more darkness the world he knows is fighting for.

11. Gethsemane: Keep Awake

The guns across the river keep shooting. The jerries are regrouping in the woods. I didn't mean to leave you. They tell me the war is over. But I can hear the guns.

Our platoon has drawn the enemy's attention. Yesterday, they shot Tom. Death is our gift for the birthday of time.

I love the sun and stars more than most. I never rest but watch the river, farms, and mountains. I know every secret of month and year.

You are goodness. Life is horror. I can't smoke because of the danger. I miss the easiness of bed and slumber.

On the third day of October, I sent you a tender sign of fall, a shadow from a tree outside my window. Do not hide your face. Do not turn away in anger.

I have news that will make humanity rejoice. Our days are hard. God's nights endure forever.

12. A Naked Boy

First Version

Spring, the garden a green fire burning the earth. Woven from fine linen, the boy's loin-cloth is too thin for the gusts of wind that still blow south from an icy north, stinging its flowery things, withering blossoms. The fig he picks from a near dead tree is miraculously sweet, a happy omen. But the moon's as glum and pocked as the bald pate of the Sadducee he serves, rising irate from a late cold bath. Scattered about the olive grove, the devotees lie sleeping, snoring, wheezing, whimpering like the Romans he also waits on, impossible to wake after a guzzling feast or a long night's carouse.

Behind him, soldiers march up the hill, the lord he adores strangely prostrate as their torches drip blood-red sparks on the bodies of his followers who scare like hares or slaves afraid of whips and lashings. Frightened, too, of what the soldiers might do with their spears and swords, the boy tries to run, but snags his loincloth on a thorn that hook-like rips it off him.

He chases after the others, loses them, finds only a cave to hide his nakedness in, resting his head on a stone slab, soon sleeping, dead to the world, coiled like a snake in a basket only a wizard's flute could coax awake and make dance to its magical tune.

Second Version

It is springtime. Gethsemane burns with a green fire. His followers sleep, two snoring, one wheezing, the youngest whimpering like a dog as it slumbers. A gentle breeze chills the air with lingering hints of an icy winter. The moon is white and pocked as the bald pate of a Sadducee. Gnats swarm over a thin pool of water gathered from dew.

After a long night's carousing, serving feasting legionnaires, wearing no more than a linen cloth as the centurion who hired him demanded, a hungry boy picks a fig not yet ripe or sweet enough to eat. One of twelve lies prostrate but fully awake as he shifts himself onto his knees and continues to pray. Behind him, soldiers march up a hill, some laughing, some playfully shaking their spears like children until chastised by their commander.

Only hares and wolves, deserters, slaves, unruly barbarians need fear their wrath. Yet at the first signs of their approach an owl hoots, a jackal yips, frogs croak huskily, liz-ards scurry over weeds and twigs, bats flap more loudly than a flock of birds flying, soaring westward, tree limbs shake and leaves shudder as winds surge before a storm, the sound of their feet pounding on clay and rock awakening the sleepers.

The praying man stands up and oddly smiles. A Judaean peasant dressed in shawl, tunic, and sandals kisses him. Another frees his sword. Tumult. May-hem. What sense to make of it? Is it abandonment? Dissolution? Betrayal upon betrayal? The chaos despair lets loose?

To chase after the others, to save himself, the boy–'neaniskos,' not precisely 'young man'–strips off his linen garment–a 'sindon,' whatever that word might mean, 'tunic,' 'shirt,' probably not 'loincloth'–as if it were being ripped or torn off him by a lusting soldier.

As wounds shed blood, Roman torches drip red sparks onto the ground. Stark naked, the boy flees, runs, runs faster into the cover of night, the darkness of Jesus and his story, and disappears, vanishes for good, as if forever. Who is he? Why did he irrupt into the gospel story only to escape, leave it as a stranger might?

I intend no comparison, analogy, translation, allegory, or myth. No similes or meta-phors. No blasphemy either, though I cherish the heresies lives conspire with to tell their ordinary stories, those that happen every day, nothing miraculous about them.

It is the enigma of why after Jay died of a soft sarcoma, Bill from shooting himself in the stomach, Baird by poisoning his body with drugs, Luke from a car crash on 441, so many friends lost to AIDS, too many to name, the unseen many of history, why they abide, why those that vanish from us stay after departure not as ghosts, but lives unfinished at the end of it all.

I know what I claim in its strangeness makes no sense. It is the inexplicable deep dark dwelling in things, in moments, that holiness clings to like a lover and will not let go. It is the mystery of joy's sorrows, the ecstasy of the unknown torn from grief. It is, yes, you, naked, unclothed, the night you left me, this senseless sem-blance, the linen garment you abandoned I hold now burning in my empty hands.

13. A Tribune's Pride

Pilate's private gardens are jeweled like fall in Gaul where in winter my men wore the fur and hides of the beast-hordes they put to the sword in woods thick with trees as Nile banks with reeds. Instead of the peace I sought, the gods have given me Jerusalem. Rome sows confusion like Carthaginian seed on all the earth it's salted. Tomorrow three more to crucify. Death will wait patiently for them, loyal as a soldier hardened by the wars. I like to watch the eyes of the crucified, how like rodents' they scan the skies for signs of hawks.

14. Forsaken

God on the cross beside himself accuser and accused do not say tribe clan nation race do not say en masse many peoples death comes one by one in the murderous chambers and locked burning barns the body-strewn rice fields the fire-bombed cities on Stalingrad's two lines the first to kill the Germans the second to shoot their own men running away one by one make no lists necessary impossible to name them all all of history recall as best you can what names you know start with your own keep reciting so my aunt the tumor in her jaw grown so large it rivaled her head my mother in her desolate hospital bed writhing in wretched pain maddened by Parkinson's choking to death my father talking of his boyhood Staten Island farm then I'm tired rolling away from me one last time or yesterday the bum in the park beating his dog with hand and stick God near infinitely far the pain like prayer perhaps if pain is lamentation expiring on the cross so lost for words he must quote a psalm forsaken into pain and dread of the last breath he breathes with us one by one or do we not breathe at all

15. The Faith of a Centurion

Fall of 'sixty-seven. Lit. 101. Three sessions late, he struts in. A carbuncula scar like a zigzag L slices his face. Booze on his breath, he chooses a desk in the right back corner.

In a Zurbaran, the boy Jesus plays at making a crown. When he pricks his finger on a thorn, Mary's bright eyes mourn for him that morning as she will weep by noon at the foot of the cross.

Larry, Guy, Brett, Kelly, then John—all vets just back from Vietnam. But only John's eyes, bleak blue, look at me as if he's always in mourning. After the semester is through, he leaves Coltrane's A Love Supreme propped against the door of my ramshackle cottage. Every night I listen to that LP. Uninvited, he brings his girls by. None of them lasts long. He makes out with Suzie on my couch, not so drunk he can't get aroused but tight enough not to care I watch.

The bar he likes best is blocks from my cottage, a place to crash when the SAE house is too far to walk to. If I forget to leave my door unlocked, he pounds on it until I let him in. Twice, he rips through a screen and breaks a window. I bandage his hand and cover him with a blanket where he lies on the floor.

Good Friday that year, he insists I attend mass with him. Next to the altar, the priest has placed on a gold stand a reliquary of the true cross. John whispers, If all the slivers taken from that tree displayed in churches round the globe were glued together they'd repopulate the forests we've poisoned and burned in Nam. Yet he prostrates himself in adoration.

After a matinee of Bonnie and Clyde, he nurses an ale at Nick's Saloon and talks about fighting for the whites in Rhodesia. Of the movie, he says, At least they know what it looks like when you shoot a man. Late April, after dating her two weeks, he marries Sarah Somebody.

Before summer is over, they divorce. When one of his frat brothers calls him a fag, he drives his fist through a plaster wall, breaking three fingers and a thumb. Stumble-down drunk, he still is wearing the splint on his hand as he kicks at my door, his t-shirt filthy with crud. I haul him in and hide upstairs. At first light, he walks straight from the shower into my bedroom, the sunshine like mist or steam gleaming off his un-toweled body. More broken letters than I had seen scar his knees, thigh, hip, butt. I loan him a new shirt. He abandons his own for me to dispose of, though I know he knows I won't or can't.

Spring of 'seventy-three. Hand in hand, he and his girlfriend or wife are hiking up the steps toward my hilltop house in San Francisco. I don't have to see his scarred face to know it's John, only his strut, his starlet blond hair, his curiously boyish bum. Just fifty feet behind them, I wait until they've reached my door before I turn down the hill to linger in a North Beach bar until I'm sure he really has gone for good and won't ever return.

One night, when we were both tight, when I couldn't guess the answer, John told me how many pieces of shrapnel still lodged in his flesh.

Thirteen, he said. It felt like a thorn or better yet a splinter of the true cross had been forced beneath a fingernail, he said, then plunged so deep in his body no human had the wits or guts to knife it out

16. *The Tomb*

Lovers of gardens lovers of humanity each time you die shine brighter each time.

17. *Sick Bed*

Unable to sleep, Joe lies restless on his bed, staring at a dead man stretched out across from him on a mattress flat as a slab in a morgue. Soon a nurse or doctor will barge in to see who in the ward has failed to weather the night.

Not Joe, who's borne worse storms than most. Fluid in his lungs almost drowned him once, tugging him back to Texas. But his bleary eyes cleared. He survived.

And now the naked phantom boy with the face white as linen sits again at the foot of a dead man's bed, his voice like a flute's, sweetly rueful as he says, What's more to fear? Here, he says pointing, or there, each time smiling brighter than before.

18. *They Were Afraid*

Sitting too proud in a crypt they find empty as his words, dressed in blinding white, the young man frightens the three women, who drop their spices. Running for their lives, they try to sing to quiet their fears.

Yet their song too easily becomes more dirge than psalm, less hymn than lamentation heard by the desolate men gathered in a room more barren than any tomb who stare at the door they've barred and the bare walls from which they've angrily torn away all images of him who betrayed each one of these mournful, disquieted men by leaving no sign he died two thousand years and more ago.

Parable of the Lost Sheep

This morning marked the eighteen thousandth
sun he has seen rise since he left his country
to journey a continent westward, a labyrinth
really, the route he took through each city,
over mountains, past deserts. A kind of maze
of his discontent, a circling back and again.
Now he sits high on a bluff of Indian Rock. The day's
near its end. His is an indigent hope. Nothing's certain.
Far out, at anchor, a cargo ship, small as a decoy,
waits to dock at harbor as promised. Waves
slap on its piles and docks. Why does water seek to destroy
a man's faith in time, in salvation? If a man saves
a sheep lost from his herd, the one in a hundred who strays,
what does it mean if he finds it flayed, skin stretched
to dry on a clothes line in Kern County? When he saw it, he wretched.

It was twilight, then, time for the fact that comes as a surprise,
like a child's bright eyes blackened by his dread of solitude.
He meant to make a pilgrimage into the sacred lives
of a people, a nation's profound interiors. The gruff, rude,
wild places of the heart. To be stunned by mountain
peaks, like cathedral domes glowing from sunset's blessing,
deserts spread out to swelter in the heat, in the glorious pain
of noon's throbbing light, of rivers half-maddened by their twisting
and turning, flooded after winter's strictures. Pretend
this man who sits high on a bluff of Indian Rock contemplating
the bay is waiting for God. He wants to know why his life must end
like the sheep he saw no one had saved. The sky's gray as stripped timber
that's weathered. Gray as the distant highway. Gray as worn rubber
or the gray tears of a child, unhappy in his home, staring out a window
as if into a mirror, the face of his father come too late to save him from sorrow.

Easter Monday Morning on Kure Beach, after Augustine

1.

A burnt-orange harvest moon
in April. Last week the seder,
four days ago the crucifixion.
It's balmy weather
on a lovely spring day here, though a cold
wind blows
in from off shore. Our deaths are foretold,
though who knows
why, even by beauty
sometimes. The Moon, the titian moon,
waits late
to set. Easter Monday dawn comes soon.
My emptiness,
is yours, Lord. Possess me,
take me, yours to consecrate.

In a crisp warm wind, dawn arrives, strong
and golden for hours.
I belong
here. This day is mine and ours.
The long night has cleansed
the skies. The seabirds' feathers, sun-lit,
sparkle like amber, gleam like burnished
steel. Driftwood,
black as a priest's
cassocks, lies scattered along the shore.
When is it not good to honor the rites? The rising sun pours out
its light like wine for libation,
like an incandescence to get drunk on,
an illumination,
a blazing monstrance for the undevout.

If it is our fear of death that makes
the world holy, then
it is holy. For whose sakes
do you hang on the cross, die again
and again?
We who perpetually must
mourn you, whom it's written you created from dust
and to dust return, what prayer should we say
to be forgiven for our lies and mistakes,
unworthiness and sin?
I think of all the days,
no, centuries we have waited outside,
your grave for you, your tomb empty Paul says
to assure us, though Mary shouts out,
afraid, "Come see," with nowhere left for us to hide.

2.

Nothing real is possible anymore. Even the tragic
vanished from earth once belief
in it died. The trick
is to believe anyway, I'm told, in grief
if need be, since to mourn
is to be torn
between life and death
anyway. The wind on my neck
feels like the breath
of a lover this morning, the world like a temple
"Tell people my story,"
Jesus preached. "How loss turns to glory
in the end when dying seems so simple
you might do it every day,
like me."

Sailors, swimmers testing the waters quietly
out of sight
on a wind blown Monday, hawk's cry,
broken shells, a night
sleepers wake
from startled by a sky
white
as gulls scattering
before the rising waves
of a sea that saves
no one, nothing,
but sunders monuments into stones
and rocks and pebbles, like the bones
tossed up from the graves
of us who are still living.

Yes, words confuse the things faith might mean.
Nothing said ever states it right.
But to be no more?
Hungry and lean,
a fox wanders the dunes, sea gulls, pelicans weak,
journey-weary,
the morning turned gray and foggy
for a moment. What is there left in life to frighten
me? How cruel laughter can be,
mockery,
an ocean, a whole world deriding me. Meek,
I would be, and innocent.
Crows forage for carnage like a man plundering trash for nourishment
while gulls strut by and preen
as if to taunt my loneliness, my abandonment.

3.

The world is forever lost to sorrow
by the power
of its constancy. High tides flow
in quickly on the narrows
of Kure Beach, tug shell shards
and driftwood
back into natural sluices,
washing the sun-warmed sands
where loggerhead turtles emerge from the seas
to lay their eggs, food
for ghost crabs. Graceful pelicans take
off from the beach so beautifully it catches my breath.
It is spring break
yet no one walks here this early. I think of Augustine's pear
how he would risk his soul should he dare

to climb with his friends over the wall to steal
it because it was forbidden
for them to do so, no motive for it but the evil
inside them, tossing the stolen
fruit to the hogs as if they were seekers more of death
than of pleasure. Laurel oak and live oak, sweet smelling bay,
hornbeam, ironwood, flowering dogwood,
longleaf pine forest the wetlands swales beyond
the dunes. Deer, wild goats, musk play
or hide in noon-thin shadows. It feels good
to be here. Green bushes and leaves flourish while the land
renews itself, spring returning with the beauty
of faith as faith might still thrive though it's been lost,
like love gone too swiftly,
like the battered shorelines storms are narrowing along the coast.

It is long past time for me to confess.
Kure is the place where
decades ago I knew,
if only for an instant, pure happiness,
where time and you
seemed to be the one
divine moment,
the blue sky over an inlet
on the Carolina coast
where we watched the sun as it rose in the west
simultaneously set
in the east, no doubt an illusion
caused as currents, cross-flowing, reversed. Yet rest
easy, I thought. So joy begins. A boy with his friend in the sun
in love on the dunes the dawn after the dawn of the first resurrection.

A Mind Too Fine To Be Violated by a Thought

An aesthetic mind. Imagine a plank Adam had cut, six feet tall,
a two by four he'd stripped, bevelled, sanding all
of it. A blank bit of lumber he had propped against a wall
like a log he had lucked on. Raw timber he had found, took

to build part of his house with, using his new tools, saw and ax,
to cut the garden's trees down with. Content to look,
afterward, at the world as it is, no urge to wander, facts
and art all that matter to him. Like the extra, leftover plank which

he had made to stand on its own, upright by a workroom door.
That he ponders often. Like a book. Looks away, back, to switch
his viewpoint, his way of reading it. Never letting it bore
him. Yet that which stood by the door soon stands upright no more.

That which leaned on a wall is sliding earthward. That which, flat,
he had contemplated, as if all a mind needed was to see the one thing,
slowly begins to topple. A thought, consciousness, contemplating
itself like a bare, spare plank cut from Eden's tree. A mind rare as it. Falling like that.

II

Purity of Heart Is To Will One Thing

The unmediated, thoughtless beauty of things. On the ocean that summer morning, a school of mackerel was skimming the surface while the sky's dawn-borne fog was the mottled gray of Sunday's rain-soaked newspaper. He's remembering his lover as he slept in his last night's t-shirt and tight Levis,

and, where they'd stood later, the scrub brush on the cliffs, bending eastward from the steady rage of winds off the sea while fist-sized rocks suddenly dislodged and plummeted onto the deserted beach. And the narrow, sandy ford they'd crossed a stream on as it trickled through reeds and rushes. Covered by

hip-high, sun-tanned golden grasses, the rolling hill they'd hike up. The snakeskin black, dilapidated barn they'd watch slowly sloughing off its peeling scales of rotted wood onto the poppy fields in the meadow below. Moments shadowed by the flickering of love, like otters sunning, frolicking in the mud of the Russian River.

If purity of heart is to will one thing, then let a gentle, surprising storm that showed them how to leave tell stories of an earth that, once it has spoken, makes no mistakes. Rain drops brief-lived as snowflakes. Or, back home, the fog, a gray web like cattails, still looming over the long day each parted in his own slow way, forgiven and forgiver.

Sweet Life, after Brahms' Vier ernste Gesänge

> Denn es gehet dem Menschen wie dem Vieh;
> wie dies stirbt, so stirbt er auch;
> und haben alle einerlei Odem;
> und der Mensch hat nichts mehr denn das Vieh:
> denn es ist alles eitel.
>   From Ecclesiastes, Martin Luther's Translation.

1. Man's Fate

His train is traveling on well-worn tracks. The man
is happy while watching it climb to a mountain
pass zigzagging like water in search of a plan,
then curving down to a river winding through a plain
fertile with wheat and ripe corn fields. Above
him are open sky and noon sun as a grackle flies
out of sight of his window, its flight like his love
for the lives he leaves behind him, the many miles
he's crossing between worlds death's divided. Why
did he not get off at a station days before
it was too late to change trains, destinations, to try
to travel elsewhere? But now he wants nothing more
than that peace which arrives from nowhere, for no reason
as the future, like the tracks he rides on, goes clickety-clack, on and on.

2. Stoicism

In Noh, when the masked male actor who plays
women's roles suffers, she does not grieve
or weep. True to the rite and its rules, she obeys
her art, lightly tugging on her kimono's sleeve.
When a priest says, "All in good time, the Lord's ways
are too deep for men to understand," is it providence
he means? That pain is a mystery that life delays
explaining until after it's over? Does it make sense,
as Heidegger suggests, to say poems sing of death
when they resound with the Being heard in Greek tragedy
or Asian theater? If poetry is inspiration, its music's breath
an exhalation of praise to an absent deity,
then, Old Man, risking the imagined great swell of the sea, think
of your faltering spirit to be peaceful as sunset when its light begins to sink.

3. In the Bitterness of Recollection

Jonquils brighter than summer, a creek, red clay,
ivy, dogwood, a May paradise mainly made
for youth. The sun's high, near noon. Cardinals, a jay,
a hissing feral cat bewitching two wrens. The jade-
glazed-green of dew-wet, breeze-blown grasses.
The dark of shade, of oak bark and its serpentine roots.
The shimmering flame blue of the lake he trespasses
to swim in daily. Paths impassable with weeds. Newts,
minnows, tadpoles gleaming like slick clay or sandstone.
His life near its ending, he lies on a bank, books, school,
work finished forever, startled to find himself left alone
by a lake waiting for afternoon's thunderstorms to strike, no rule
to shape its lightning and wild winds. How unlike late life is to a boy's
peacefully repeating his nighttime prayers that he be blessed with its
new joys.

4. Charity

The Preacher says, What befalls beasts befalls men.
A man shifts his head to face his bedroom wall,
its shades stained sleet gray, its windows wide open.
His body sags, or might as well. He feels skeletal-
calves, thighs, pecs, arms. Few of his friends
survive him. There's no one to turn to. In the depths of dread,
his every thought's on death. What, if anything, transcends
what comes to all? What the ancient preacher said
of beast and man is tragic. Nothing lasts of peace, bodily
pleasure ever after. Yet he is happy listening to the late music,
so final, by Brahms, even if its heart is chilly, its spirit wintry
as January winds whistling over a moonlit, unpeopled, mythic
land. By a will stronger than his, its music sings on and on in his head:
that a life might find heart's ease in time despite what The Preacher said.

Sparrow

In deepest night, a man—ever restless, lying alone in bed, unable to sleep—
sees himself being shadowed on his ceiling as if he were watching
a flickering movie screen as he walks down a street, its buildings steep
and sheer as cliff face descending into sea-surge, a nocturnal darkening

of a body blurred by the sun denied it until out of nowhere a lone sparrow
lights on his shoulder where it perches content, staying for a long block
or two until it flies away so fast and high his tired eyes cannot follow
its flight. Yet, as he reaches the edge of the city's empty park, a flock

of sparrows circles above his head mimicking a festive ring like dancers
leaping round a May pole. As he holds his arms out, opens his narrow,
bony fingers, the same, tame sparrow he knows from the markings below
its wings rests in his hand as it sings its song clear as night fountain's waters

burbling, rippling, a silvery trilling as if it were happily improvising, no guide
to anything, anywhere, solely to delight in, until, serenade done, it flies
out of the sky through a crack in the ceiling, an illusion the man tries
to believe is real if only for a moment more since he hopes outside

himself he still might find some sense to give his unloved life, some answer
to it, as if in a sparrow's song he could hear after it's disappeared, belied
by his sorrows—like a touch of a hand, a kiss on the forehead before he's died—
what peace night thoughts might offer yet, and this its vision and winged messenger.

Rites of the New Year

1.

At dawn's low tide, the ocean is calm. Gray,
drifting clouds. Along the shoreline,
young people chant hymns to the first day
of the new year. An aqua sky. No sign
of more rain. The boys and girls wear
bright red flowers in their hair for the rite
to Laka they are performing: to the sea,
to life and love, to their homeland, Hawaii.

A ragged, worn man watches from a dune, out of sight,
his skin so palely white and faded his skull
looks like a death mask. Youthful
bodies, lit as if with the light
of paradise, with their own fearsome gaiety,
gleam like the sun off the sea
as he sways as if dancing to the young ones' studied ritual.

2.

This beach is no place to learn silence.
Waves crack like ice
floes breaking. Near sunset
the winds turn to violence
at a storm's onset.
Plovers scurry
in ritual circles
mimicking a dirge
above the pounding waves, the lee-
ward shrieking of gulls, the surge
of the sea. Miracles
in a sense,
how one hears the earth's sudden
stillness and the quiet of sun and sky
after like mourners left breathless, grieving together in mute ululation.

3.

Two hawks soar over bluffs, climb
higher, perch in a Monterey pine
on a precipice. Sheer cliffs. Boulders
battered by encroaching waters.
From the headlands, pelicans fly
through mist into a darkening sky.
Passing by, hikers head to Land's End,
read the winds, vanish round a bend
in the trail. By the Gate, foghorns moan,
intoning, like Russian basses, their ritual drone.

Like a river in a Noh play,
a shallow stream flows
near us stretched out like a long white cloth that knows
all a ghost knows and will not say
what it is that's flowing seaward under the crescent-moon bridge.

4.

The January sun is reflected by sea
like a wanderer
on a journey,
by the turbulent waters
smashing his light
to thousands of pieces silvery
as fish scales,
golden as coins
ejaculated from the loins
of a god. In the end of the day, it never fails,
the ancient belief in divinities. As the sun
sets, a rite
of summer repeats itself in the early winter sky,
twilight burning beyond the obvious horizon
as if it is shining with the glory of life lived at the limits of reason.

December 7, 1941

His father and mother are basking in the sun-porch
with its views of the park, its windows frosted over,
lustrous as lamp shades in the afternoon glare. Birch
trees sweep their branches across low eaves, winter-

barren and spindly. His father smokes an apple pipe
as he scans the editorials in the Sunday paper.
His mother is sewing opal buttons, gleaming like ripe
olives in sunshine, on a blouse she's bought her daughter

who is lying in her upstairs bedroom reading a book
about a teen girl and her mustang. His parents are listening
to the New York Philharmonic concert, Shostakovich's
First, under Rodzinski, too biting and ironic for them. "Look,

Dear," his father says. "Robins in the birdbath!" The last stitch's
sewn on her blouse for her daughter's party with its fancier
buttons. It is intermission. The Japanese have been bombing
Pearl Harbor, an announcer states flatly, battleships sunken,

planes destroyed, many lives lost. "Oh no," his mother says,
to her husband. "War in our lifetimes again." "Again,"
her husband repeats, "so soon after the last." It is near day's
end. In his mother's womb, their son, too, hears the bitter news,

early in his gestation, truths of a world he'd never choose
to be born into many months later, something in him, his genes
perhaps, already mournful as if a life begins the moment history intervenes
in it, though his mother smiles as she feels his first stirrings inside her.

Lvov

Nearby were wheat fields, green meadows, flat lands, sloping hills,
creeks, streams steadily feeding a river sparkling
in sunshine, barns, ancient farmhouses, stone mills.
Now that world is invisible. At the edge of woods, burr-bearing
brush, web-tied vines are entangled with dead ivy. Many villages
have been eradicated from every map, forgotten as their people.
We, too, will be no more soon. Yet sit by me. See the sad visages
of the families in photographs taken after the fin de siècle?
Each one stands proudly erect and somber in rooms
gray, smoky from age, subdued, flame-lit, smelling of candle
wax and the musty bindings of thick books, all the furniture
weighty and dark as if carved from stone. Some grief looms
over them, some unknown dread that has made them unsure
of the future. Notice how despair is visible in the knots and tangles
of their lampshades, rose and gold like porcelain bowls. Imagine
the sorrows conveyed by faded wallpaper, the stark white and black
of their clothes, cold and gloomy as winter woods, their mirrors' fine
carved frames too fanciful, too old-fashioned to survive attack
again, week after week. Under fire, the protective glass, as it cracked
or broke, tore or ripped apart every photographed face or mirrored back
and well groomed head, leaving their lives blurred, erased, as if they had lacked
all reality by being defeated. Which is what violence means to achieve, to be
  unspeakable.

Three Degrees below Zero

It is a January night in Vermont. There's a broken down clunker
of a car in it. An Arctic fury's might. That winter's worst. A tree
is in this story, too. A curve. A slick road. A crash. Drunk or not.
Deliberate or not. A man who later wived and did not want to be.
Black eyes. Black hair. Rich black ruin of a beautiful boy.
Lost or not. No one knew, not even me who loved him in snows
high drifting like those he'd seek in Colorado later, the joy
of cold nights and freezing air, a man's breath like ice. Clothes
partly off, he'd snuck his hand across my thigh as, both tight, we lay
side by side in the shadows of a backroad snowbank in upstate
New York he'd driven his sports car into after a gray Saturday
of hiking in woods close by and drinking at the Inn we'd quit too late.
Three degrees below zero should numb a body from its desires. Yet we made love
anyway. Unzipped anyway. Kissed, his lips cold, his hands on me icy without gloves.

Right at first light, back in the frat house late, not speaking, he gave
me Vidal's The City and the Pillar to read, dog-eared, his favorite
novel, he said, like a secret to be kept. I watched him shower, shave,
dress, leave for an early class, all in silence, all else, despite
what had just happened, left unsaid for good. He'd soon flunk
out, intending to, I guess. No word, no note, he just went,
took off, telling no one, leaving no message behind. The bed he bunked
in was stripped, desolate. I lay on his mattress. Longed to find the scent
of him still in it, as if possessed by him, by the snow and cold air
of him, his wintry ways as we'd hiked through woods behind the college,
into a darkness where no one could see what we might uneasily dare
to do again even if we could not do it, the snow enticing, like the edge
of our world, stark, moonlit and desert bright. Years after, I wrote him a letter
in Vermont. He wrote a longer one back. "My silence is saner, if not better."

Yet he also told me how, on his trek west, outside a Denver truck stop
a guy tried to pick him up, admiring him, his beauty, his sharp motorbike.
The man'd wanted to fuck his ass bad, he'd said, like the macho top
he pretended to be. C. wrote me all he'd wanted to do was strike
back somehow. Hit him. Prove him he wasn't like that at all. And yet inside,

he couldn't be sure. Back home, he'd married, hoping to hide
in New England ritual, in a wife's safety, as if that could stop it, be all
he'd need to do to erase the past, the past he'd abandoned, left to die
before it had had a chance to live. But it does survive, the life of us, as I recall
it always with a shiver, the chill in my bones, we both feverish, the night sky
transparent, star-filled, so memorably white after a day's hard snow it gave
me false hope. Here, two lifetimes later, far away, bitter winds off the ocean rise
from the sea like voices of wrecked men in distress no one dares rescue or save,
drowning men afraid of being dragged deeper into the mortal coil of their unlived lives.

Maybe he died a suicide. Maybe not. No one seems to know for sure.
The story is now sixty years old, our time together like a mad fantasy
no magic spell or good luck charm or sleeper's dream could cure
me of, haunted as I am by all my living dead. Long ago, I saw in a movie
directed by Jacques Tourneur, set in the tropics, how men every night
beat drums for those who cannot die but none of the living can say
are truly alive, men whose eyes can't see, yet possess keener sight
than theirs. The island's rites dictate that whoever dwells by light of day
must carve images, simulacra, effigies with hatchets and sharp pen-
knives, then beat their drums relentlessly, hour after hour to conjure
the undead beachside to die, who cannot swim but unlike living men
will not drown. Not zombies but those desires our lives must let endure.
The woods where C. still walks beside me are dark, the sky as hidden. The moon is low,
yet shines with a glow that glistens off his bared body as if forever, brighter, more pure
   than new snow.

After Listening to Bach

Its close counterpoint astounds, line upon line.
An osprey dives into an Oregon river
abounding with rainbow trout to dine
on again and again while noisy fox squirrels chatter

concealed by plush foliage of cottonwood and ash
whose strict limbs creak in winds while the water
flowing west babbles on even as, with a loud splash,
the osprey plunges into the stream once more,

a writhing fish, as it flies off, caught in its beak:
spare fragments of a transitory scene which memory
alone can release from time, play like a score
composed of many themes resounding together,

the way the sun shimmers on the surface of the river,
its light twice real in late August's clarity,
apples ripening, squabbling chipmunks drunk on berries,
a garter snake slithering through cattails and weeds' leaves

as if there is something in nature so confident it can speak
all at once, late summer flourishing, north country wet, fir
trees, reeds dripping with spray, the early morning dew,
and the rain, the sudden rush of rain from the storm as it passed through.

An Early Morning Walk on the Day after Christmas

Scattered along the Marin headland from the Gate
northward, south far out as the western horizon
down to Pacifica, the crab boats' beacons this late
into a long night of rain are dim, hazy as stone
lanterns in a Japanese garden gentle showers fall on,
blurring the light. Fierce winds form new dunes
by piling sand off the beach onto the ice plants
next to the highway. A lone crow, beneath the moon's
dim light, plunges as if torn out of the sky, weightless
as waves' foam, the ocean's churning white water far
as the eye can see premonitory of more storms, I guess.
Tiers of cement blocks, boulder breakwaters, bastions
against floods, have been stacked at the foot of cliffs, tar
black and slick like clouds in the east delaying dawn. What enchants
me most about the world is the baffling art of it, the beauty of a single blazing star.

Dreaming Homeward

1.

My father often haunts my bedroom late at night,
meaning to console me. "What you should
have done, you did not do." I know. Shadows
from my past chase after me. Family. Friends.
There's little time left to make amends, right
the wrongs of a life neither true nor good.
In the dark, other ghosts rail at me, strike blows
against my pride. No dream ever stops. It merely ends.

2.

See their appalling, shattered bodies, like anemones,
calla lilies, parrot tulips, orchid and leaf, lovely
in their white ovoid vases, their outré faces,
defiant expressions, their myriad beauty,
the dear ones in my dreams who come to save me like my father,
the petals that fall from them dropping beside me, flower by flower.

3.

Yes, dreams confuse things,
nothing said ever right.
Far off, someone sings,
far off and out of sight.
A bell tolls. How cruel
laughter can be. Mockery.
Shadows through a window.
A long ago day in school.
A too long gaze in a pool.
Another fib. Another lie.
Unable to cry. Nothing to show
for it. I stand on a boulder
at land's end studying an empty
sky like a blank piece of paper
I write my name on for you to read
and thereby see me.

4.

Oh, dark companion of my childhood
who is saying goodbye as he fades
into evening while I recall how good
and kind he often was, my shades
drawn as I watch the moon shine
through, not that its light can matter
but the images it throws like a sign
on my ceiling are my ghosts as they blur.

5.

Take care of your ghosts, I'm told. Offer
them common pleasures
as they float over
the world, wanting back in.
Nothing assures
you of their love, looming over your head, your long lost twin.

6.

In a dream of home, the window that breaks
if opened, the room that it takes
a life to be free of, the door
I've locked, unforgiven: the more
I dream of you the more my heart aches.

It is a sleepless night that makes
me visit my past to fix mistakes,
my way there closed, as before,
in a dream of home.

Mower, hoe, trowel, shovel, saw and rake.
I've gardened years for my father's sake
and for my mother's the daily chore
of polishing the parquet floor
I'd promised to clean before daybreak,
as I dream of home.

A Poem Made from Poems Written When I Was Sixteen

"You can't repeat the past." "Can't repeat the past?" he cried incredulously. "Why of course you can!" He looked around him wildly, as if the past were lurking here in the shadow of his house, just out of reach of his hand.

1. Winter Rain on a Meadow

At the first crack of breaking ice,
twelve crows, four to a pole,
take flight, swoop by me twice
until they perch again, four to a pole.

Whenever two clouds collide, the sky
buckles, fracturing day. Cloaked
in dusk's disguise, the golden eye
of the sun darkens to copper and bronze.

Falling hard since early morning, the rain
leaves pock-marks on the gray-
green mud of the meadow.   Plane
trees' limbs weave webs that drip in the creek.

2. Summer in a Field

The red clay dust penetrates
everything After a soaking shower,
the viscous coat of it separates,
cracking into broken, asymmetric discs.

The sun bakes fields, hills into a thin
glaze of earthy orange, the days so hot
rusty leaves fall from trees, tin
barn roofs blaze white, and wild flowers'

petals waft and drift in the wind
like bits and pieces of confetti tossed
into the air near the woods, flying like winged
slim things dancing in space over the fractured earth.

3. Heavy Snow on a Golf Course

In Wordsworth's "silent seas of hoary mist,"
hungry birds cannot touch
ground. Our joy is in nakedness kissed,
cold, simple lives comforted by a few blankets.

No solid life is here, yet I might walk from land
to water to sky, to free my body
in the midst of winter so I can stand
on a creek that, by freezing over, dared me there.

4. Vacation in Maine

What do we want of each other?
Hike the clean limits of Maine.
White rocks, sails white, clear
white sea. Fog free, the sun washes us both.

The wind blows through my window.
Early light blurs my books and desk.
Low mist with the melted gray glow
of candle wax rolls in, but not to stay.

As I wade through lapping waves, I see
the day unfurling at dawn
like the sails of the boats on the lee
side of the cove, billowing at first wind.

5. Walton

Flight is grounded in basic certainties
of structure and, of course,
well-known banalities of form.

On his family's farm, a hawk swoops
in its modern air
as if in search of somewhere higher,

a purer element. Chafed by its beauty,
strict as Walton's, as bereft of choice,
I watch it soar, dappled, wimpled in the cryptic air.

Of Prayer

1.

A surfer in his wet suit is like a puppet
in a shadow play, the sky a ceramic
plate, the tumbling sea at sunset
a Japanese print, the beach slick
and matte as an ancient silk screen.
Yet the world is ceaselessly changing.
I heard a monk say the real world
is not its thin surface, but the thick
one that lies beneath it. "Life, you see,
floats on the stream of being. A sun
shines best off what is dark." I
managed once in a river's roiling
waters to touch bottom. To free
a reed from mud to prove I'd done
it. To bring it to the surface. To show you why.

2.

I remember the chill night that I watched you
standing immobile on a treeless hill
in west Marin, staring toward its view
of the sea, clouds and winds still
as in a painting, the sky flat black
and calm as the ocean, empty
and quiet. When you looked back
at me, you were serene as a marble
statue, a runic stone. All was ours
in that darkness. You approached me.
I wanted to join you, let the hours
go as they might, but you were fast
passing from sight. Must nothing last?
You were already fading into night
the night we started. That beautiful. That immortal.

Company, after Stephen Sondheim

Times Square marquees highlighting anxious faces, neon
signs flashing, stop lights shrill as spots
on cop cars, a squat, dust-sallow moon
bulging between high buildings. A sweaty night, lots
of people, too many on the streets hanging about,
sitting on stoops, resting on fire escapes,
sticking their heads out of windows in a drought
that never seems to quit. Inhuman heat reshapes
a city, makes its air breathless. A crowd leaves the theater
reviving an old hit musical. They've just heard a character
in the show, out of his own heartbreak or the ordinary
sorrows of being alive, sing to each of them intimately,
lover to lover. Now the party is over. They are each alone,
longing for company. And they know what he means, of what
he sings, these theater goers cast back on the streets on a night unbearably hot.

Rainbow

A boy is playing with the hose in his father's
garden, making it rain, making a make-
believe play rainbow in the mist as he waters
the roses, splashes spray on mower and rake

and over the living room window which mirrors
his face, or so he thinks, staring back
at him from inside. The sun is so hot it sears
the grass in the yard leaf-brown from long lack

of rain. Magnolia petals fall at his feet
from force of the hose's power, delicate
and white as lace or crochet, heat-
tipped with the rust of decay, as if summer is satiate

with life's generosity. Old now, he sees
outside his window, as a storm forms over
the ocean, evening breakers, trying to seize
back day's last light, tumbling, crashing onto shore

while dozens of rainbows arc above the rumble
of the waves, the white water in which gull
and sandpiper play as children will in the spray
of a garden hose, in the mist after a summer shower.

Immortal Gardener

The dawn sun's majesty hides behind Santa Monica hills
where the sky shines like a shield beaten from gold.
Azaleas, fuchsias, bougainvillea, yellow daffodils,
passion flowers bloom like a story I've often retold
of you the first time I'd held you. You'd scratched
an eye, its cornea slightly torn by rose thorns
while you pruned its owner's garden. I'd watched
you many times at work, the butterflies, swarms
of bees flying about you, perfumes of scotch broom,
dusky fennel, lemons dazzling as the vibrant petals
your touch had turned ravishing, each made to bloom
more beautifully in your hands until a mad rose clawed
at one eye that morning I drove you to the doctor's, the patch
he gave you to wear after like a pact between us, like the thatch
of hair, mutinous and piratical, that fell over it, glorious as your marigolds.

Spring Sonata: The Light May Sees By

At a break in the clouds, a plait of pale blue
from the sky caresses a field of sunflowers,
a blue as soft as the lake their petals float in.
The beauty of day never asks you
to believe in it. It pours
down on you like rain
in May, like grace. In your garden,
snails slip past fence rails on their snail-
slick bellies toward roses whose thorns
won't save them without you, whose petals open
wide under a sky
the watery blue of your eyes. Grass tickles your toes.
Hose spray trickles through your feet. Dandelions
shimmer in a warm wind that's sifting through pines
as the forms of things mutate into spring. Wherever May goes,

you follow. Tadpoles to frogs. Crayfish breeding under
rocks. Incense of budding magnolia and wild roses,
of leaves darkening, of honeysuckle
summoning you. Clouds like sails unfurling. The raspy chir-chir
of crickets in the early morning. Swallows
swirling. A black-horned beetle
fierce in its armor
making its deliberate way through a patch of sassafras.
Wet bark from a stand of loblollies
redolent of wood smoke, the last trace of winter.
All this I stare at from my bedroom window
as you tend the hibiscus beneath the shade of a white-
walnut that's thick-limbed as an oak trunk while I spied

on you, watched you sip cool water as sunlight
sparkled off your body like a first illumination, like the light
of shimmering things I'd seen before when a fishing boat's stern

plowed the ocean like untilled earth while terns,
black-crowned, red-beaked, white
and gray feathered, circled over the choppy
Atlantic. I stood alone, on a rock, a promontory
until something inside me
was seized by sunlight, by its flashing
off their wings as they dived and dived, splashing,
beneath the waves happily
satisfying their hunger. It is the body inside the body
like the deep dark recesses
of oceans we'd possess within us that glow with bioluminescence,
strange sea creatures, florid in their wild loveliness,

like your garden in early May you so ardently cared for,
fresh leaves sparkling like jade glistening,
winged seeds drifting,
rising heavenward in morning's breezes,
dwarf silver threads, boxwood sparkling
with late dawn dew, green lynx spiders weaving
webs among milkweeds' tall, firm stalks,
regal white and pink lilies
by the fish pond, the green world you'd made before
I knew you, the body
hidden inside your body, the one I'd spy
on forever if I could, or guess about, like red-tailed hawks'
nests in trees too high for me to climb or the spiky
spruce needles or bark chips

floating downstream from your creek steady as ships
toward harbor.
I was a boy who enjoyed basking under
a perpetual sun
in the viridescent gleaming of spring,
in May's precise intensities, clarifying, sharpening

the colors and hues of flowers, trees, everything,
like the fluttering milk white anise butterfly flying
lustily about you, as if to tell me:
This is reality,
Peter, all of it you will ever need to see
like a gift from the sun,
from the heart of light that shone
for a moment through his sweat as if light itself dripped off his body,
wet as a swimmer's, the fiery luminosity that burned you with its transient passion.

A Few Notes

1. The translation of lines 313-316 from *Aeneid*, Book VI, is mine.

2. The three words in Greek after the title of "After Herakleitos" are Ethos Anthropos Daimon, for many years translated into English as "Character is Fate." But that translation violates Herakleitos' "saying" in all sorts of ways, among them by substituting a psychological observation for an ontological assertion about the essential, non-propositional identity of the three.

3. The Latin in "Exile" means, "The death of Publius Ovidius Naso." In CE 8, the poet of the *Metamorphoses*, which Ezra Pound regarded as his bible, was exiled by Augustus from Rome to Tomis on the Black Sea for what Ovid called "carmen et error," a poem and mistake, accusations of licentiousness being part of both. One might regard his exile as an example of Augustinian puritanism and censorial cruelty, not unlike that which happens frequently in our own time. Ovid died in Tomis, never having returned to Rome, in CE 17 or 18.

4. The first of Brahms' *Four Serious Songs* takes its words from *Ecclesiastes*, 3: 19-22 in Martin Luther's translation from the Hebrew. In "Sweet Life," I cite only the first stanza of the song.

 19 For what happens to the sons of men also happens to animals; one thing befalls them: as one dies, so dies the other. Surely, they all have one breath; man has no advantage over animals, for all is vanity. 20 All go to one place: all are from the dust, and all return to dust. 21 Who knows the spirit of the sons of men, which goes upward, and the spirit of the animal, which goes down to the earth? 22 So I perceived that nothing is better than that a man should rejoice in his own works, for that is his heritage. For who can bring him to see what will happen after him?

Some of the greatest recordings of the *Four Serious Songs* are Kathleen Ferrier's, Hans Hotter's, and Janet Baker's.

5. The passage quoted at the beginning of "A Poem Made from Poems Written When I Was Sixteen" is, of course, from *The Great Gatsby*.

Peter Weltner taught Renaissance poetry and modern British, Irish, and American literature at San Francisco State University for thirty seven years. Twice awarded O. Henry prizes, he has published six books of fiction, short stories and novels, and, since his retirement from teaching, many books and chapbooks of poetry. For nearly twenty years, he was part of Five Fingers Press and Review. He received his A.B. from Hamilton College and Ph.D. from Indiana University and has lived in San Francisco since 1969, most recently in the Outer Sunset, steps away from the Pacific, with his husband, Atticus Carr. His most recent books are In the *Half Light*, published by BrickHouse Books in Baltimore and *Bird and Tree/ In Place, Scrapbooks Mappings of My Country*, and *Woods and the City*, published by Marrowstone Press, Seattle. *Crow-Black Stones and a Flock of Crows* is forthcoming from Agenda Editions in the U.K.

www.ingramcontent.com/pod-product-compliance
Lightning Source LLC
Chambersburg PA
CBHW022020290426
44109CB00015B/1246